Out of the Ashes, WE RISE

TAMYKA SILVA

ISBN 978-1-64569-090-0 (paperback)
ISBN 978-1-64569-091-7 (digital)

Christian Faith Publishing, Inc.
832 Park Avenue
Meadville, PA 16335
www.christianfaithpublishing.com

Printed in the United States of America

Foreword

As Tamyka's oldest sister, I've known her all of her life. I have watched her experience many heart wrenching trials and throughout them all she has come out a conqueror. There were times that fear gripped her and tried to immobilize her, but she always would internally fight to overcome until it manifested in the natural. As I sit today reflecting on various memories, I am humbled that she asked me to write this foreword as I totally admire her perseverance, persistence and willingness to do what's best for her growth in spite of the naysayers. Tamyka is a beautiful woman with a beautiful soul that wishes the best for everyone she comes in contact with. She amazes me because she is always looking through a different lense on how her various testimonies can help someone in need; to encourage them that although the current pain might be tumultuous there is a rainbow on the other side. God has already blessed her with Henry, her wonderful husband and her awesome daughter Destiny and two additional boys, Henry Jr. and Richard. I am excited to see what else He's going to do through her life as she is Already soaring above the ashes!!!

I'm sooo proud of you Sis,
Tishawa Howard

A woman of great faith is what I see. At first sight there was no doubt that Tamyka was a chosen vessel of God. As all of us, she has had her share of trials and tribulations; however, the way that she handled each one of them made me notice that the Holy Spirit was truly operating in her broken life. Tamyka always gave God the glory, honor and praise through every test and trial that I witnessed her to go through.

When asked how she was doing, her response would be and still is "GOD IS GOOD." I recall three horrific incidents in her life that would have probably sent most people into a sea of no return depression, BUT GOD…the fatal accident of her young husband, the unexpected murder of her dear and close friend and her miraculous escape from the terrorist attacks of New York City's World Trade Centers where she worked. Tamyka's faith and trust in The Almighty God, supernaturally had her bounce back with amazing strength and a powerful testimony. Not only was she restored but she came back stronger, wiser and more determined to be a forerunner for The Lord. Her attitude reminded me of the scripture in Romans…ALL things work together for the good to those who love the Lord and are called according to His purpose. She wholeheartedly displayed it working together for good every step of the way; even through fear and questions.

PURPOSE was the key word that I felt described her journey. I believe through it all she realizes that God had a purpose and plan for her life, and I'm sure it may have looked cloudy many of times; however, every event of tragedy drew her closer to God and pressed her to be even more attentive to His calling for her life.

As she continues to navigate through life with Grace and Mercy on each side, I stand with encouragement, wait in expectation and marvel with excitement to see the golden opportunities of real-life experiences she will share with so many all over the world; the mission that she has obviously been assigned.

Losing loved ones or surviving the hand of death; did not mean that God had turned His back, rejected or had forgotten, nor was He finished with her. It clearly paints an outstanding composition that A Great God was preparing her for such a time as this. We should look forward to reading every chapter of this book keeping in mind that God is still working miracles EVERYDAY!

Soror Cynthia S. Caldwell

The Start of it All

" It's cold outside", I thought. My parents bundled us up and took us outside to play in the snow. A normal five year old would love the fact of running out and playing in the snow. Well, not this one. I did not like the snow at all. We lived in northern New Jersey. It was cold more than it was hot. Our family was always coming together. We are first generation Americans. My family are from Jamaica. My parents told us it was time for a change, and they decided to move to Florida. As my parents and their four kids at the time migrated to South Florida, I was thinking in the back of my head how excited I was to get out of the wretched cold weather. In the same breath, I had to leave all my family members and friends that stayed living in New Jersey and New York. My cousin Tisha was born a day after me and our parents would always treat us like we were twins; birthdays together and everything else. It was hard for me to leave them behind, but I looked forward to knowing I didn't have to put on so many clothes anymore to go outside and play. We arrived in Florida, and immediately started school. I met so many different people. It was a little culture shock, because we were always in our Jamaican circle of family and friends. However, now we were surrounded by different walks of life, mostly Hispanics. On the weekends, we would pack up and go to Haulover beach. I thought this was like a Jamaican hang out spot, because the amount of them that were there at the beach with their families. We experienced being in a Rastafarian culture. This is a religion that a lot of Jamaicans practiced. As a little girl entering school it was weird for me to explain this culture. It was like I was living in Jamaica in America, if that makes sense. Our house resided in the suburbs of South Florida. The front of the house was your typical Floridian home; however, in the back, we had like a mini farm. There was a big chicken coop, with our chickens and roosters. We also had a big tree with a tree house built at the top. I never really wanted the friends that I met come to our house and see that we were raising our own eggs, and sometimes our chickens were actually dinner. In the late 70's and early 80's, it wasn't popular to have dreadlocks, and all the adults in our circle had them. Some of our parent's friends made their kids grow them too, but I begged my mom not to do that to me. I didn't want to add any other attention to me that would cause me to be bullied, so she obliged. Entering elementary school was enjoyable; it helped to meet all the kids in the neighborhood. One of the requirements in Florida was to take a second language. I had a burning desire to take Spanish. I loved the language, and thought it was quite easy. Every day I would go home and practice with my neighbors; however, one day one of their uncles were mean to me and said that the Spanish they are teaching is not correct Spanish. I became afraid to practice with them after that, but still continued to study every year. Soon, it went from four of us to six kids. We are all two years apart. My oldest sister Tishawa was the protector of us all. She was not only older than us; she was our defender in everything. She would make sure we were well taken care of. The only thing I didn't like is that I had to always get her hand me downs. She would wear an outfit on Monday, and then my mom would wash it, and I would have to wear it on Tuesday. What a struggle that was. I am the second child, so Tishawa and I naturally formed a bond; almost as if we were twins. Then came my brother Rhasaun. He is an artistic person. He thinks outside the box and could draw anything really well. Next Taneike, the fireball. She was very tiny and feisty. She wasn't afraid to tell you how she feels. She didn't let anyone run over her. I honestly envied that side of her, because I was shyer and held back my feelings inside. I wanted the fire but was too afraid to embrace that character. I remember when this one girl wanted to fight Tishawa. They were in the 6th grade, and Taneike was in kindergarten. Everyone lined up outside the school yard to see the fight, and the girl went to try to hit my sister, and here comes Taneike hitting her with her lunch box and fighting back. She was only in kindergarten, but she wasn't letting anyone attack us. We always laugh at how she was so fearless, as this girl that was a giant in my eyes try to attack our oldest sister. My next sibling is Tesfa, he was the quiet son. All of us babied him. Then, finally was Amayae, she was quiet as well. So Tesfa and Amayae were babied by all of us. However, Tishawa, Rhasaun and I were considered the "big kids", and Taneike, Tesfa, and Amayae were considered the "little kids". My mom would pack us up in her Mustang, along with our cousins Tasha and Michael, and go get some Cozolli's pizza. Then we would take a ride to Miami International Airport, sit outside and watch the airplanes take off and land; while eating our pizza. It was so many of us; she had to find innovative ways to keep us entertained. So after being outside watching the planes, we would go inside, and then the real fun began. We ran all over the airport. There was no such thing as security like it is now. We would run up and down the escalator, and throughout the airport. We would have fake people paged on the paging system. It was the funniest thing ever. I would pick up the phone, and the operator got on and said, "Hello, may I help you?" I responded, "Yes, can you please page my sister Penelope Poopenheiper, she's lost." So then on the loud speaker would hear, "Penelope Poopenheiper, Penelope Poopenheiper, your family is looking for you. Oh the laughs and the fun that we had. It was better than the playground. After hours of pranks and running around, we would head on home. All of our cousins loved to be around my mom because she would just let us run and have fun. We would go outside and would ride our bikes, play mother may I, hopscotch, hide and seek, school, kickball, and so many other games. We made sure all of our homework and chores were done so that we could go out and play. Because my dad was very serious about the Rasta way of life, we couldn't eat pork, so he read every label, before we could eat any-thing. For me it was difficult to explain why we couldn't eat pork or anything that contained lard, like Oreos or hotdogs. He wasn't allowing us to eat any of those things. I remember learning in school about goldilocks and the three bears eating porridge, and then expressing that we ate porridge as well. Why did I say that, I was the joke of the class? This wasn't a typical American breakfast, and I didn't know how to explain what porridge is. Neither did I know anything about typical American dishes, such as grits or collard greens. I was trapped in our Jamaican culture. It felt good when summer time would come, and we would head to Jamaica for the summer. We would spend time in the country running up and down the mountain, through the gully, climbing trees and just enjoying our culture. I realized that they would go to the beach on the weekend, and we would have fish and festival. Yum, this was so good. One day I was outside looking at the goat, and my cousin was telling us that this would be the goats last day. I thought he was teasing. Well nope, he wasn't. Later that afternoon, I watched them kill the goat. He was running around, head cut off. What a shock to my brain that was. The next day we sit down for our curry goat dinner, and I was saying to my aunt how delicious it was. Of course, my cousin chimed in and said, "remember that goat that was killed yesterday, you're eating him". My face was so startled. I didn't know whether to puke or just deal with the fact that he tasted good. I continued eating, and just didn't try to put too much focus on what I saw. Going to Jamaica was a yearly occurrence until I was thirteen. As the time of middle school approached, my parents didn't want us to go to the schools in our area, so they sent us to schools in North Miami Beach area. I didn't want to go. We had to get up extra early in the mornings just to be on time for school. Tishawa and I was signed up for Highland Oaks Junior high and the rest of my siblings, were signed up for Highland Oaks Elementary school. Most of the kids that went there were of the Jewish faith. I had a sigh of relief, because now I felt I didn't have to explain why we don't eat pork, because they didn't either. It wasn't a topic of conversation. I still was taking my regular Spanish classes, along with piano. I loved my piano class. When I started to play, I felt so relaxed as if I was in another world. I made so many friends. Denise and I became really good friends and would always hang out. Later, I met Malika and Shamique. Denise, Malika and I would cheer at our local optimist club for the football team in Ives Dairy. It was in the 80's, and those days, people would have dance crews and not gangs. I remember Malika, Shamique and I forming a dance crew called the Boot Ta Booty crew. We would inspire to dance like the videos we watched. At home, Tishawa, Taneike, Tasha, and our friends in the neighborhood, would form another dance crew call the Slangems. Dancing was big in the 80's, and everyone was trying to out dance the other. My mom would take us to the skating rink, but we didn't tell her it was really a teen party. Luke Skywalker "Uncle Luke" was the DJ and Two Live Crew would perform. It was the life. My father had this pickup truck. We named it the "ghetto truck", and he would drop and pick us up from the skating rink. In school, I met another friend in my computer class named Crystal. We hit it off from day one; and our name was Twice Da Spice. Every day Crystal and I was together. We were inseparable. She became my best friend, an additional sister. I took her to meet my family, and we all got along well. Her brother and Rhasaun became good friends and formed their own bond. It is very rare that you will find a friend that you can trust, never judges and can relate to. She understood me, and I understood her. For fun, we used to eat onions as apples. We always strived to be different than other people. One day, we made a bet to not comb our hair, wear mismatching clothes and shoes, to see if we would still get attention. It worked. These were some of the fun things that we enjoyed doing. We didn't want to be in the box. On the weekends, my siblings and I would either hang out with my grandparents on my mother side or my grandmother on my father side. My dad's father died when he was 16 in a car accident in Jamaica. His father was actually a descendant from Cuba. So my father learned Spanish from his grandmother. After, his father died, and later his grandmother, they never really pursued the language.

Every Sunday my grandmother on my mother's side would take us to church. It was actually an adventure for us. We we went to the Salvation Army church and it was different then what my friends would describe their church was like. It actually was a time for my siblings, cousins, friends and I to have fun. We would attend the Sunday school class, and as soon as church started, we would all escape across the street to McDonald's to get our hot fudge sundaes with nuts. We would make it back in time for the adults to get out of service. They had no idea that we had left. It was our ritual every Sunday. At that time, I knew about Jesus, but I really didn't have any kind of relationship with him. I just loved going to meet friends and have our escape. Every summer the Salvation Army would have different youth away camps. I couldn't wait to go. I remember being thirteen years old, and my siblings, cousin and friends wanted to go to camp. We were all excited to have some fun without our parents for the week. Camp was about five hours away, and we were enjoying ourselves on the bus anticipating our destination. Wow, we get to Camp Keystone, and it is amazing. There is a big pool with slides, different cabins, a canteen, and many other features. We knew that we were going to have a lot of fun. The girls of course were in separate cabins from the boys. Every morning at 6am, there would be a loud speaker across the camp with a song "Good morning, Good morning it's time to rise and shine.' Oh how we hated that sound, but that was time to raise the flag, pledge of allegiance, pray, breakfast, bible study, and my favorite part was free time. We would go to the canteen and get our ice cream, and all the good snacks that wasn't served at meal times. One day we were having our service, and the counselor was talking about the Holy Spirit, and that day was the day that everything changed for me. As we were singing and learning about the Lord, something came over me. It was like this cloud of Love. Love that I never experienced before, and then they had an alter call. At my church there was always one, but this time it was different. The Love I felt kept pulling me to the altar. So I went. I started to cry and cry. Everyone was asking me what was wrong, but I couldn't describe what I had felt. The amount of love that I felt that day was indescribable. I wanted more of that Love. I was crying, but really overjoyed with what I was feeling. God had poured out his love for me that day, and I truly felt he was hugging me. I still remember that feeling. I felt the change and the shift in my spirit. The first time that I experienced true love. Jesus kissed me, and it felt so good. I desired to know him more, and I would try to study and learn more about him. When we got back home, I would sit around and listen to my grandmother and her friends talk about the Lord. Then I started to hear about David and how he had a heart after to God, so I wanted to study him, and wanted that for myself as well. That year was the beginning of something different, but also for many trials. One of my favorite time spent, was playing the piano. We were preparing for our concert at the University of Miami. I was so excited and nervous at the same to be on stage playing with an orchestra. After school, I got dressed in my pretty pink dress and heels, called my uncle to come and pick me up since my parents were working. I was all ready for my big day. I envisioned being on that stage for our big debut. My uncle came, got in the car, didn't put on my seatbelt, and off we went. I was telling him we had to hurry and get there so that I wouldn't be late. All of sudden boom, I jump out the car, and all these people were staring at me. To my surprise, we were in a really bad car accident. I didn't remember a thing. I started yelling, "I am late for my show, and I need to get there". People were asking me to calm down. I said, "No" I need to get to UM. Then I looked down, and my dress wasn't pink anymore, it was red covered in blood. I didn't realize that my head was open from hitting the windshield. You could see the flesh and bone in my elbow, because all of the skin came off, and there was a big gash in my mouth. In that moment, I realized that I would never be able to perform at UM or experience being a part of an orchestra; instead I was rushed to the hospital in an ambulance. Despite the pain I was feeling on the outside, I felt more pain that I didn't make to that concert. My parents arrived at the hospital, and to our surprise I had no broken bones. However, the doctor's spoke to my parents about amputating my arm since it was open, and you could see the bone. My camp experience taught me how to pray, and I asked God to not allow them to do that. I told my mom that I didn't want that to happen. She spoke to the doctor's and they said that they will have to do it. Then there was this Cuban doctor that came in, and he said to my mom "I can save her arm". He advised her to make a paste with brown sugar, betadine, water, and wrap it. The doctor's found out that this one doctor advised us to do this, and threatened to fire him, but he told us to keep doing it anyway. We would do this every day and the flesh started to come back on my arm. I couldn't move it, but it was amazing to see the flesh growing back. They stitched up my mouth and cleaned off the glass on my forward. I still have all three scars from that accident. I believe God sent that doctor to help me heal. That year my parents also separated, and we moved with my mom to an apartment complex. I still couldn't move my arm, and the doctors said it would be many months before I would be able to. One night I was praying to God with my mom and her friend, and I felt the Holy Spirit again as when I was in camp, and all of a sudden, my arm flung up in the air, and I was moving it. I then saw the Lord clearly, rock me in His arm. It was a glory that I never felt or experienced before. I knew in that moment that God really is a healer, and all I needed to do was to believe that he could heal me. Years passed, and now I am in the tenth grade, and my mom now decides that she is moving to New Jersey with my younger siblings. My older sister and I didn't want to move, so we decided to stay with my dad. We wanted to stay with our friends and school. We weren't up to change. My mom re-married, and when I was planning my sweet sixteen party, we were introduced to our new sister, Sophia. She fit right in with the rest of us. Both of us are the same age, and we love her as if we shared the same natural parents. She lives in Canada, so we would spend time with her on holidays and summers. As years passed, my sister Tishawa, left for college in West Virginia. Everyone started to slowly migrate out of Florida. My senior year, she called and asked me where I was planning to go for college, and I exclaimed, "I would love to go to Clark" in Atlanta since it was known for their Business program. I was into Accounting and wanted to pursue that degree. She then said, "If I fill out all your paperwork for West Virginia, get you accepted, housing and make your schedule, would you consider coming?" I didn't believe her, so I said, "sure". In my mind, I was like "yeah right". Do you know that in two days, my sister called saying that she did everything that she said and to pack my bags. So, I did just that, and off to West Virginia I went to venture in my new college life. We arrive to West Virginia and stop to get gas. I went inside to pay, and the guy said, "Welcome to West Virginia" in the most southern twang. I laughed so hard and couldn't contain myself. We get to the campus, and all kinds of emotions were racing. I was excited, nervous, and scared all in one breath. My sister worked it out so that I didn't have to stay in the freshman dorm, but live in the on campus apartments with her instead. It was bittersweet, because I had more freedom than the average new student, but I didn't get to experience what the average freshman went through in a dorm. I first got there thinking I was going to study accounting, and then I changed to Elementary Education. College life with my sister was so much fun. We were always hanging out, and I would always find myself with her friends and Sorority sisters. I really was intrigued by her sorority sisters, and wanted to join myself; however, I had to wait until my sophomore year. I met so many people from different states across the United States. It made me realize how big the world was. There were so many different perspectives that this Miami girl didn't realize. I was into Miami bass music and loved to dance. At every party, you would find me on the dance floor. I would also socialize with a lot of people. Most of the people that I would hang out with were on the basketball team. It was the spring of 1993, and Delta Sigma Theta sorority of Alpha Delta chapter announced that they were going to have an initiation process for more ladies to join. I was so excited. Everyone knew that since my sister was already in the sorority, that naturally I was interested as well. I didn't waste any time signing up, and I was accepted. I was able to meet some of the most beautiful women to share this journey with me. There was Shanice, Shelly, Kelly, and Tomica. For the next weeks, we shared a bond like no other, and on March 5, 1993 we crossed into Delta land. We were all so excited. Through our chapter, we helped build a home with Habitat for Humanity, food drives, parties, and many other community related activities to service our neighbors. It was one of the best college experiences. I was able to be a part of our annual homecoming step shows, and just meet amazing people in our and other Greek letter organizations. Not many are afforded the chance to be in college and active in so many things.

However, I had time for everything, but God. I stopped going to church. Not because I didn't believe, but because I was drained from having to go all the years prior. I would just read Psalm 23 or say the Lord's prayer, thinking that it was all I needed. My faith was there, but I felt I wanted to have fun without feeling any guilt of doing what I wanted to do. So, I called on God when I needed him, but there was no true fellowship. Time after time, he would be there for me, but I made no real time for him, except on Easter, Mother's Day and Christmas. As long as I fulfilled these requirements, it was good enough for me. At least that is what I thought. In the spring and summer times, I would sometimes visit Miami and New Jersey. Fast forward, and it is time to graduate, and I wasn't ready to move to Miami, so I decided to try a life in New Jersey. After college, I moved back in with my mom. It was a rough road, because I was used to living independently with my sister, and now I am back home with my family. My younger brother and sisters were still in middle and high school, and I felt I was much more mature than that. Trying to find a job in education was challenging, because I was told that every state you live in, you would have to take the teacher's exam. I passed the exam for West Virginia and New Jersey, but I couldn't fathom taking it for any other state that I may move to. So, I started to think what other field would be of interest to me, and I decided to try Telecommunications management. So, DeVry University have this program for an Applied Arts of Science degree, and I signed up. "Really," I thought to myself, you go from a Bachelor's to an Associate's degree, but I needed something that didn't require a test to get a job. This was a scary step, because I didn't know much about the field; however, I learned to love it. I was able to not only learn the ins and outs of a computer, but also about programming telephones as well. The program was so broad, that there was a choice to either pursue the phones or pc. DeVry had a great lab, that I was able to get my hands on both. I learned about the PBX systems, as well as taking apart a pc and fixing it. This was a different world for me. They also promised all students that would have job placements upon graduation.

The Calm

It was December 1999, graduation was approaching, and we were so excited. The night was set. Family and friends were present, anticipating the procession of the graduates. It was my second degree; but this time in the field of telecommunications management. One of my classmates started talking to me about the Lord and inquired where I went to church. I advised that I didn't have a church, so he invited me to his church in Perth Amboy, NJ. I re-dedicated my life back to Christ, and started Bible studies to re-establish my relationship with him. I would read and study more, but still desired to enjoy all the activities geared towards my age group. Later my youngest sister would introduce me to another church in Rahway. I would go from time to time, but really enjoyed where I was currently fellowshipping at.

The very next week, a group of us were interviewed for our first *real job*. The women of information technology (IT) landed a job on the fifty-ninth floor of One World Trade Center. It was so exciting. That was where it all started. Instantly, four of us bonded, forming our version of Charlie's Angels. There was the beautiful Moroccan (Samiya), Colombian (Christina), African American (Paula), and me, the *JaMerican* (short for Jamaican American). It was exciting going from the fifty-fourth to the fifty-ninth floor while setting up and assisting. It felt like we were on top of the world—at least it appeared to be from that view.

We were always together at work, every lunch, and sometimes after work. We formed a bond like no other— always there for one another, learning and growing and enjoying the New York way of life. Samiya, a Moroccan; Christina was single; Paula was single too, and I was dating.

Summer would come and the best part was coming downstairs at lunch with the *angels* and watch different celebrities perform. The plaza was so big, and always loved seeing the HOT sign lit up from Krispy Kreme donuts. Many people would pass by as we bonded with each other, laughing and having a good o'le time. Then the Yankees won the World Series, and the parade was right in front of our building. I thought to myself, *How blessed I am to witness so much greatness at work.* I had a house in New Jersey, I worked in the best building in the United States, and I had a nightlife with some amazing friends. Wow, this was the life! Every day, we would go to lunch at different ethnic places. Working in New York City was so exciting for us. The city that never sleeps was the place that I loved to be. We ventured from downtown to uptown Manhattan. The bright lights and enormous amount of activities, made me love being there even more.

Fast-forward to the end of August 2001, my brother and his wife had their baby. Everyone was so excited until they found out that he was born with a heart condition and needed a heart surgery. Since my brother and his wife couldn't make it to the surgery, my sister and I went to Pennsylvania to be with baby Akil. The doctor came and said, "Surgery went well, and Akil will have a long life." He was then transferred back to a hospital in New Jersey. Every day, the family went there to see him.

I returned to work and was on my usual route going to work on the train and that was where I met Sheila, who I was riding with for the past one and a half year. She asked me, "What do you do?"

I said, "I am a desktop support specialist."

"Really? Where?" she said.

"The World Trade Center."

"Wow! You do?" she asked.

"Yes, and I love it."

"You're not afraid of working there?" she asked.

"Absolutely not," I said. "Why would I be afraid of working there?"

She said, "Because of the terror attacks back in 1993."

I then said, "They hit it once. They are not stupid enough to hit it again."

"Well, I would not work there," she said.

I smiled and said, "Well, God has not given me a spirit of fear, but of power, love, and a sound mind like in 1 Timothy 2:3, so I trust I am good."

We both agreed and transitioned to other topics until we reached our destination.

I arrived at work, and our manager called the four of us in and said, "The company is purchasing all new computers, so we will have a move on the weekend of September 8, and we were are all required to be in attendance to set up the new computers."

It was the morning of September 8 and the four of us met up at the World Trade Center, going floor to floor hooking up computers. We were laughing, joking while making sure all clients were getting set up. Suddenly, I saw a small commuter plane outside, and I got my friend's attention. "Hey ladies, look at this plane. Wow, it is eye level! How cool is that?"

We all stared in amazement at the view of the Hudson and the small plane. Then reality kicked in, and we went back to work. Later that evening, my cell phone rang. It was my cousin from Miami on the other end. "Hey girl, what's up?" she said. "I am coming to Manhattan on Monday, September 10th in the evening," she said.

"What part of Manhattan?" I said.

She said, "At the Federal building downtown, across from the WTC."

"Oh, perfect," I said. "Let's hook up for lunch then."

"Sure, no problem."

The Storm

There was a constant beeping of the alarm clock at six in the morn-ing. "*Aww*! Please no, I don't want to get up." Thirty-minutes later, I jumped up realizing that I was going to be late for work. I got dressed in my white blouse, black slacks, and new high-heel boots. I was ready for that morning of September 11. I walked out-side toward my car and said, "*Aww*, the weather is so nice and sunny. It's going to be a beautiful day." Then I jumped in my blue Jeep Cherokee, and off I went to Roselle Park train station. While on the way of my ride on the NJ Transit, and then to the NJ Path trains, I was thinking how lovely the weather was to be in fall, and I couldn't wait to get to Manhattan. I arrived at 1 WTC around 8:00 a.m., stopped and got breakfast at the cafeteria, then headed to my desk on the fifty-ninth floor. The elevator would get you to your destina-tion in less than two minutes. When I walked in, I saw my friend/coworker. "Good morning, Samiya," I said. Then I proceeded to my desk, started the computer, signed in, and packed my belongings away.

There was an issue with one of my supervisors, and I remem-ber writing a letter in response to the things that he said and did. I looked at the clock, and now it was about 8:40 a.m. The phone rang. "Hello, this is Tamyka. How may I help you?" I asked.

"Good morning, Tamyka. This is John, and I forgot my badge at home. Can you come downstairs and sign me in?"

"Sure, give me a few minutes to wrap something up, and I will be down to get you," I said.

Not wanting to lose my train of thought, I continued to type all the details in the letter, not realizing that five minutes had passed. "*OMG*, I forgot about John!" I hit the print button, got the letter out of the printer, and went to my chair to put the letter on my desk, then boom and then boom again. I could hear the floor falling. My chair flew to the other side of the wall and then back to my desk as if I was in a slingshot. "Samiya," I yelled, "what was that? Are you alright?"

"Yes," she replied, with both fear and worry in our minds.

The PB announcement came on. "Please evacuate the building repeatedly."

I said, "Samiya, let's go."

"No," she exclaimed with fear and doubt in her mind as she asked what happened.

"Well, I don't know where you are from, but where I am from, you get the hell out and ask questions later," I exclaimed. So I finally got out of my chair and looked around my desk for any belongings that I wanted to take with me. I remember only having about $13 because I changed purses the night before. I walked around the corner to Samiya and said, "Come on, let's go."

She again exclaimed, "I am not going anywhere."

"No, we have to leave now," I said. "Give me your hand."

She yelled and said, "No, I am staying right here." I said,

"Well, I have to go. You know that I am two months pregnant, and I don't know what's going on." So I proceeded to the elevator and guilt began to grip my mind as I was leaving my good friend behind. My heart was telling me to go back and get her. I did turn around to get her, and to my surprise, she was with our IT director Lewis. Whew; that made me feel better. I said, "Are you alright?"

He said, "She's fine, don't worry I will help her to get out."

"Okay," I said. and I proceeded to the elevator again. I ran into another coworker, Karl. "Tamyka, you can't come this way," he said.

"It is raining jet fuel." I said, "Okay, what I do now? I am on this fifty-ninth floor and pregnant."

He said, "Take the stairs."

Still, all I could hear was "Please evacuate the building" over and over again on the PA system. I went to the staircase and told myself that I was in good shape, and I would just run down. To my surprise, it was crowded, and I was going nowhere fast. *Oh brother*, I thought. So with no other options, I proceeded to join the single file line down. We were walking down the steps to the right, as it was standard to keep the left available for firefighters, police officers, and any other emergency crew. It seemed like it was going to take an eternity to get out, because of the amount of people in the stairwell.

Growing up in Miami was pretty much hot year-round, but that particular staircase was so hot that I wanted to peel my skin off. I couldn't bear the heat. In my mind, I was thinking, *if hell is this hot, I will do whatever it takes to stay far away from there.* I was really small, so people had no clue that I was two months pregnant. The heat was getting into me and everyone else around. Each moment, I would think of my family and unborn child, and if I ever would get a chance to meet them. To not know your fate, as if your passing in the wind is very frightening. My life felt as if it was hanging on only faith. I had no control, and that was scary. I had to put 100% of my trust in the Lord. However, people were trying to make the best of our current situation by laughing and joking about it being a bomb, and that we would have two weeks off before coming back to work. No one actually knew what was going on, but they did say it reminded them of the attack in 1993 on the towers and how they were off for two weeks.

Because I was in college at the time of the first attack, I thought, *Surely these people knew by experience that it wasn't a big deal,* so I chose to trust them and remained calm. People were actually celebrating and making plans for their expected time off not knowing how dreadful our situation really was. There was so much peace in that staircase. As I think back now, it was hard to fathom the terror outside because of the calmness, laughter, and peace going on inside. The story of Peter in the boat with Jesus came to my mind in how Jesus was sleeping while the storm was raging.

Immediately, Jesus made the disciples get into the boat and go on ahead of him to the other side, while he dismissed the crowd. After he had dismissed them, he went up on a mountainside by himself to pray. Later that night, he was there alone, and the boat was already a considerable distance from land, buffeted by the waves because the wind was against it. Shortly before dawn Jesus went out to them, walking on the lake. When the disciples saw him walking on the lake, they were terrified. "It's a ghost," they said, and cried out in fear. But Jesus immediately said to them: "Take courage! It is I. Don't be afraid." "Lord, if it's you," Peter replied, "tell me to come to you on the water." "Come," he said. Then Peter got down out of the boat, walked on the water and came towards Jesus. But when he saw the wind, he was afraid and, beginning to sink, cried out, "Lord, save me!" Immediately Jesus reached out his hand and caught him. "You of little faith," he said, "why did you doubt?" (Matthew 14:22–41 NIV)

Following Directions

The Holy Spirit was present, because I felt a strong sense that everything would be alright, and this was not yet the time. It seemed as if the other people around me felt the same way since no one was trying to stampede on each other while trying to get out of the buildings. God works in mysterious ways because had people known what was going on outside, I honestly think more people would have perished that day. Thousands of people passed through the World Trade Center on a daily basis since it was a main hub for people to catch the train as well as a mall located at the ground level. However, everyone was quiet, respectful, and calm, to say the least.

I met two ladies that seemed to know each other. We started talking about ourselves and trying to find ways to pass the time as we continued to walk down the unbearably hot staircase. In Revelations, the Bible talked about the lake of fire, and it had to be hotter then what I felt. The thought of feeling that intensity of heat made me overjoyed that I knew Jesus as my savior. I shared with them that I was two months pregnant.

"Oh really, wow!" one of them said.

"Well you must be very anxious."

"Absolutely," I said, not trying to show too much fear.

We were all trying to make calls on our cell phones to see what was going on, but there was no service.

"What are you going to name your baby?" one of the ladies asked.

As she saw that I was starting to really become doubtful, and she wanted to ease my mind.

I said, "If it's a boy, I would name him Destin, because he was destined to be here; and if it's a girl, I would name her Destiny, because she was destined to be here."

"Wow, that is really nice. I pray you will meet your little one," she said.

Then she asked, "Do you have any other kids?"

"None, this is my first."

"Well, congrats and good luck," she said.

It worked. I became calm, at least for that moment, until someone finally got service; and they said a plane hit the building. Fear started to grip in again, and I said, "A plane." We all started saying it must have been a commuter plane. My mind started to drift as I remember when we would fix the computers in the executives' office and how we would see small commuter planes flying close to the building. and it was like *Wow that is so nice*!

So we all decided that it was a commuter plane. Both my sister in law and my unborn child soon to be grandmother were on a three way call. I could hear Linda yelling, "Tamyka, are you alright? Are you alright," in her Southern twang.

I said, "Yes, I am fine."

"What happened? What's going on outside?"

Then the phone just hung up and there was no more service. I was wiping off the sweat, and the two ladies were saying, "Does anyone have water. She is two months pregnant."

To my surprise, someone had closed a cold bottle of water, and they gave it to me.

"Thank you," I said. Each step downward felt like I was going nowhere fast. I wanted to leap over all those people to safety, but it would not have been right. So, I just kept walking and praying to myself.

By now it was past 9:00 a.m., and someone's phone rang. All I could see was a great fear in their eyes as they listened to the person on the other line. He then proceeded to say that the other tower was hit too.

"Guys, I think we are under attack," he exclaimed.

So all the peace and joy we had instantly turned into fear and doubt. I was holding so tightly to my stomach while thinking and praying. "Lord, please help me to get out of these buildings so I could meet my baby."

In all of the fear and doubt, there was still calmness in the air. No one tried to rush. People were being very helpful and respectful to each other. This was the first time that I saw love in New York City and not the constant hustle-bustle. Then my childhood memories started playing through my head: the times of playing around in Miami with my family and friends. All the family gatherings, birthdays, summers in Jamaica, New York, etc., kept racing through my mind.

My mind shifted toward college at West Virginia State University (WVSU), to all the wonderful people that I met and then joining Delta Sigma Theta Sorority and all the fun and bonding we had. I started thinking about the good times after college with family and friends in Jersey and New York. It was like I doubted that the Lord would get me out, so I went down memory lane. As much as death was in front of me, life kept reminding me that this was not it and would not end like this. Suddenly, I woke up from my trance and saw firefighters. They were all young and quite handsome. I knew it was not the right time to think about this, but I am only human. The look on their faces actually concerned me even more as we clapped and cheered them on for their bravery to go up the stairs with all their equipment; then we proceeded to go down. They had the look of "I know this is my last day, but I rather die helping than watching all these people lose their life." For that, I would be forever grateful to firemen. Thank you again for your service. We often forget that when people take those roles, they are literally risking it all for someone that they do not know. This reminds me of how Christ intended us to be to serve others, better than ourselves. However, he knows us, and desires the best for us.

We were on the fifth floor, both planes had hit, and we finally realized that it wasn't a small commuter plane but a big 747 plane. At that moment, I realized that this may very well be my last day, but I continued to try and hold on to the little faith that I knew that I had. The Lord promised that all we need was mustard seed faith, and a mustard seed is very small. If you have faith as small as a mustard seed, you can say to this mountain, "Move from here to there, and it will move. Nothing will be impossible for you" (Matthew 17:20, NIV). That was all I could give, but I knew that in return He would move that big mountain from me. Anyway, I saw this very large man in a wheelchair at the stairwell. My heart sunk in because there was absolutely nothing I could do to save him. Everyone was trying to run past him just to get out of the building. What was even more interesting was that people ran in a single file line down the stairs without pushing one another. The firemen of course went to assist him, but I didn't stay to see what happened. The unknown of his and their fate will always remain in my heart.

My two newfound lady friends said, "Hey, why you don't break your heels to your boots so you can run?"

"Silly," I said.

"No. I spent $89 on these boots." I refused to break them and proceeded to head down. What was I thinking?

I got to the plaza level with a sigh of relief and hope in my eyes. To my surprise, I didn't recognize the plaza anymore. I felt as if I was in a dream. *Where am I?* I thought. *Is this not the WTC?* It was full of so much smoke and debris that I thought I was in a war movie. I could hear sounds as if there were bombs everywhere. I turned to a police officer and said, "Hey, can I go outside this way?"

"No," he exclaimed, "it is raining debris and bodies."

And as soon as he said that, *boom*, a big white man's body smashed on the ground. I screamed so loud that I thought the whole Manhattan heard me. I just started to run and run until I found an exit. I exited the building and saw a big fireman outside loudly advising people to head north. I looked back and realized that was the same fireman on the TV. My two lady friends appeared and said, "Hey, Tamyka, there is an ambulance right there. Let us walk you over there." Then they grabbed my hand. I felt the Holy Spirit speak inside of me in that very moment and say, "If you go that way, you will lose your life, but if you head north and not look back like Lot's wife, you will live." Luke17:32–33 said, "Once God has called you out of the darkness into His marvelous light, do not look back. Remember, Lot was afraid to escape to the mountain lest some evil would overtake him. It is written." So with great force and determination, I looked up and saw that great big ball of fire coming from the towers. I snatched my hands away from those ladies and yelled, "No." They looked at me as if I was crazy. That was the last time I saw them. I don't know what happened to them either. There were so many people in the crowd, looking in amazement at what was going on. There were kids outside in strollers, and all the people there were watching history in front of their eyes in amazement. I ran into a few of my coworkers. And they said, "Tamyka, stay with us." All I could hear was that still small voice that said, "No, head north." So that time I politely said no and kept heading north. It is important to listen to the voice of God. Some people call His voice your conscience, but it is the Holy Spirit. He is constantly speaking and guiding us; just as we seek directions on Google maps. It is our job to listen. You will be surprised how much He speaks with signs and wonders.

Walking through the crowds of people was not an easy task. People were literally just in a standstill. Up in the sky, I could hear and see fighter planes flying over us. I ran to a group of my coworkers, standing and pointing in amazement. We all gave each other hugs. Feeling overjoyed that we were out; however, unsure of the others. One of them asked me to stay with them, but I felt the Holy Spirit instructing me to keep moving north. So, I gave my good luck and byes, and kept going north. The craziest thing is that it was many people just waiting for the inevitable; even with kids in strollers. As much as I wanted to see what was going to happen, the Lord was directing my path. As I was walking through the crowd, I realized that I had no friends or coworkers to find my way home with, since they wanted to stay. It became a lonely walk north to what seemed an unknown fate. I got out of the crowd and finally got in touch with one of my friends and told him I was okay, and he shared with me what was going on. That was when I found out that there were four different planes that attacked the United States. While he was talking to me, I saw a crowd of people running toward me, and I said, "Oh my gosh!" He was looking at the TV.

Suddenly, I said to him, "I have to go, and then I hung up the phone."

Then I heard that still small voice again, "Don't run straight, turn to the right down the street and run there instead." The Lord was my compass. He guided me the entire time. I just needed to listen to His voice. It stood still, but I could not discern its appearance; a form loomed before my eyes, and I heard a whispering voice (see Job 4:16). That was when I realized that God was always trying to make an escape for us, but were we really willing to listen and obey His commands? It could mean a matter of life and death.

Later, I realized that the people were running because the first tower fell. I thought another plane had hit. I didn't know until I finally got home that the towers fell. Despite all of this, the day was beautiful. My adrenaline was kicking in. I didn't feel anything except hunger and thirst. I had to make a decision to spend some of the money on a cab or food and water. Thankfully, I ran into some very nice people that were willing to pay for a cab with me. By then I was in Little Italy. The cab driver was very nice and didn't turn on his meter or even charged anyone. People were very nice and warm that day. No one cared about race, religion, political views, sexual orientation, or anything else. People were just human. It amazed me how out of the ashes, we had risen with God in the midst. I got to midtown Manhattan with the hopes of catching the NJ Transit home. But of course like everything else, there was no transportation in or out of New York City, so we ended up getting off from the cab on Fifty-fourth Street instead. I wanted to be as far north as possible, still thinking that the further north I go, I would escape danger; but it was not the case. Suddenly, the reality of New York City being an island was what was on my mind. The only way in or out was by boat. So I decided to get something to eat while remembering that all I had with me was $13. I found a sandwich place and that became my meal. All I could say was "Thank you, Jesus, for keeping me this far."

While talking with the restaurant staff, I found out that there were people using their personal boats as well as ferries to take people to New Jersey. However, those trips were near Thirty-fourth Street. The only choice that I had was to head south toward those boats. *I can do all things through Christ* (Philippians 4:13) was what I kept thinking and proceeded to head south. While I was walking to a destination of hopes to get home, I bumped into a young lady. We instantly started talking, and she became my company for the next twenty blocks. Of course, the incident that was taking place was the topic of conversation. She boldly said, "I wonder what all these Christians are saying now. Where was their God in all of this terror? He let so many people die today," she said.

I looked up and started laughing to myself. I had a quick inward conversation with the Lord.

I said, "You are funny, putting me with a woman that doesn't believe in you."

The Lord whispered back to me, "I knew you before you were formed in the womb. For such a time as this, I have placed you here."

Then my personal conversation with the Lord ended, and I was back to my conversation with the lady. I said to this young lady, "What is your religious background?"

She said, "I am an atheist,"

"Funny," I said, "I am a Christian."

Of course her eyes were wide open with a sense of slight embarrassment.

I said, "Well let me tell you where God was during all of these. You are looking at a miracle. I was in the 1 WTC on the fifty-ninth floor when the first plane hit. Also, I am two months pregnant."

Her silence was deafening. "There was calm in the staircase, and I don't know how many people passed. However, I believe more people are alive because of God's peace and protection." I could tell by the look in her eyes that she was overtaken by the words that were coming out of my mouth. It was the Holy Spirit speaking through me to her. I was no longer afraid and was trying to get home real fast. My concern then was to minister to this soul. His commission is my only mission. Remember, I felt how hot it was in the tower, and I was able to describe it to her knowing that I didn't want this soul to feel even remotely what I felt. I felt love for this young lady and told her the love of Christ and how He was all over the city. His peace was there. I felt safe in His hands. I remember describing all of what I encountered to her. Just like that, we reached the boats. She gave me a hug and said thank you and good luck. God took my eyes off of the terror going on and inside of me, to use it for His glory. I didn't know if she came to know Christ, but I was glad that I was able to plant a seed in her that day. We talked so much that I realized we finally reached the harbor off of Thirty-fourth Street. There were boats and ferries everywhere filled with passengers. People were coming to NYC with their personal boats from all surrounding areas and states to carry people off the Big Apple. The line was very long to get to the boat; however, I kept telling people I was pregnant and just got off the building; therefore, I needed to get home. To my surprise, everyone was very nice and allowed me to skip the line and get on the next charter boat to New Jersey.

There was an eerie silence on the ride to NJ. If you ever saw the movie Titanic, and how the survivors were on the boat, waiting for assistance, as well as, overcome by the disaster, then this was the same feeling that I saw and felt that day. I still didn't know that the towers had collapsed. Finally, we got to New Jersey, and every charter and city bus were there waiting to take people to the Meadowlands where family members were told to pick up their loved ones who survived.

I remembered the father of my unborn child coming to pick me up. I shared my experience with him, and that was when the news of the towers going down was relayed to me. I had so many emotions that were flying in my head. I was sad, overwhelmed, angry, nervous, anxious, thankful, guilty, etc. I didn't know what to think. *But, Lord, why me? Why am I still here? Why did I have to experience all of this? Why did all these people have to die? This is not fair.* Then the peace of God came upon me, reminding me of how people were at peace inside the towers. He started to speak to my spirit to let people know that He was there and how many people became calm because of Him. Many people died, but many more people lived because they were late, clueless to the extent of the events, didn't come to work, and because of many other stories that I heard. God was there the whole time. He didn't do this to America. He wasn't punishing anyone. That was all a lie from the pits of hell. The Lord actually was the ram in the bush. (Exodus 3:2) Many had risen out of the dark ashes of that awful day in history. He was a very present help in the time of trouble. (Psalm 46:1) He also whispered the countless of people that did pass that day that accepted Him and went into glory that day without feeling any pain.

God is a good god. He wanted me to keep my mind stayed on Him and His beauty, so it would be at peace. (Isaiah 26:3) Later that night, I went to the hospital to make sure that I didn't inhale any smoke. *Why did I do that?* They took this very long needle and stuck it in my hand to check for smoke inhalation. I screamed so loudly I thought the entire hospital heard me. I still feel the pain just by thinking about it. All the tests came back negative, thank God.

The next day, it was very eerie and weird in NJ. I didn't believe that the towers were gone, so I made my mom drive me downtown to see them for myself. I started to cry and thank God all in one breathe upon seeing how I could've been there in the tragic grave site. My manager called to relay that I could stay out of work for two weeks; however, we had to come meet at the Waldorf Astoria to account for all the employees. We all arrived at the hotel, and it was a weird feeling. All the lawyers and upper managers were very humble and grateful to be alive. We did end up losing one employee.

Trials and Tribulations

During all of this, my mind was still focused on baby Akil, who was still in the hospital. Things started to get worse then better, and then we got the call after one month that Akil lost his battle and went to be with the Lord. I couldn't imagine what my brother and his wife were going through since I was face-to-face with death and was also pregnant. It was a very emotional time for our family as could be expected. I had to eventually return to work full of emotions.

Manhattan was different for the next coming months. There wasn't any hustle or bustle but only kindness. It was something I never felt; and all churches all over were packed with attendance. People were trying to put everything into perspective. Fast-forward and I finally got to meet my baby. I was at church, worshipping and in the spirit, and there was suddenly a kick, and I knew. I was rushed to the hospital, and the next day I had my little girl. As promised to the Lord, I named her Destiny since we were destined to be here. I was so afraid of dying, that I didn't know how to live. The airport wasn't really far from my house, and one day I heard a plane that was really loud, so I ran under the bed shaking. My cousin Tasha came to see if I was okay, and that is when I noticed that I suffered from trauma. As much as I believed in Jesus, I confined myself to my own prison, because of my fears of 9/11.

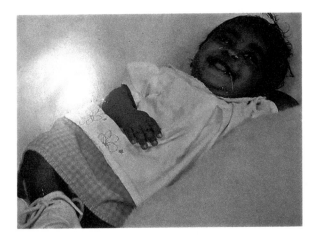

After several months of maternity leave, I had to return to work. We were then in Times Square, and there were constant bomb threats. It was very challenging to leave my baby home, not knowing what attack could happen next.

A year later, I no longer worked for the company, and I decided to use my teaching degree instead. I started substituting in my area, and it was great. I could walk to work as well as be close to my daughter. One day, I was in the teacher's lounge and I was talking to one of the aides. We started talking about the 9/11 attacks, and she told me that her brother was one of the firefighters who lost their lives and how she wanted to know that he died in peace and as a hero. I looked at her and said, "I was there."

I told her my story. She was amazed.

I said, "God sent me to let you know how peaceful it was inside and how I looked at those firemen as heroes for going in to help people as we were trying to get out."

It was a big crying fest between her and me as we hugged and thanked each other for encouraging one another. The Bible tells us, that He knows us before we formed. (Jeremiah 1:5) The Lord knew that day was going to come, and He made a divine connection that was needed. This was another time that I said, "God, instead of saying why., I want to know who?" My question was "God who can I help, and who need to know that you are real. You are the very present help in the time of trouble (Psalm 46:1)." I stopped trying to look at what I went through on that day about me, but I was trying to reach the person that needed Him more than me. This attitude of my trauma became my ministry. I now prayed that God would send the hurting people my way. In order for a seed to grow, you need soil, water, location, sun, etc. During that time many different things can happen, but if given the right properties, it will rise and grow. Life isn't about keeping your mind on your trials and tribulations, it's about taking those experiences and helping someone, as someone else help you.

In my darkest moments, I looked around and so many people were there to help me along the way. It's in those times I understood that God never intended for me to go through it alone, so I had no choice but to trust the process and rise. That was a healing moment for me.

Destiny was three years old when one of my students mom invited me to her son's birthday party. That was where I met him. He had his little girl, and I had mine. It was an instant connection.

Tish and I dated for a couple of years. His daughter was three years older than Destiny, but they got along well, and everything was going great. It was the fall of 2006 when I got a phone call that one of my sorority sisters that I pledged with had passed away from her long battle with lupus. Surprisingly, her name was also Tomica. We all took the drive to Michigan to attend her funeral. My other *sands* a term for sorority sisters that I pledged with) Kelly and Shelly were also there. It was a bittersweet moment: seeing ladies that I loved dearly and knowing that we were saying goodbye to Tomica. We reminisced on good times at school and leaned on each other for support during this difficult time. One of the saddest moments was to bury a close friend and namesake. That was the first time I had ever felt such a deep pain.

A couple of months later, Tish proposed to me, and I said yes. We took a family trip with the girls to Florida to see my family for Christmas; it was a great time. I remember hanging out with them at the beach and many other places; we even attended my cousin's wedding. The wedding date was set for July 7, 2007, in Florida. The pastor that was set to officiate the wedding told us that when we get back to NJ, we should go ahead to the justice of the peace and get legally married so that when we have the ceremony, we don't have to worry about the legality of it. In January 2007, my sister and her boyfriend came to NJ to visit, and we all hang out in the city. A few weeks later, the phone rang and my sister was crying on the other end. her boyfriend was murdered by his friend. I felt horrible for her. I didn't know what to say or do. He was just here. How did all of this happen? About a week later, my mom called and said that my cousin was murdered in the same area. The month of January instantly became a sad month for my family. The only good news was that my sister who lost her boyfriend found out that she was pregnant. Unfortunately, her unborn child would never get to meet his/her dad anymore.

Tish and I took the pastor's advice and applied for marriage in the courts. On February 15, 2007, we got married in the courts. No one but my parents and siblings knew that we were married because we wanted to have our ceremony. The following week, Tish wanted to buy a motorcycle. Everything in my fiber was against him getting it, but I finally caved in and said okay. I wasn't comfortable with him getting the bike, but it was one of his dreams.

One day, he was in the kitchen and expressing his feelings for me. It was nice, but it also felt like a goodbye. I couldn't explain it, but it was like he knew something. The next day, he woke up from a dream. He said he saw someone on a white stretcher and sheets covered over him with blood everywhere. He was very scared. I asked him who it was, and he said he didn't know. His answer didn't seem convincing to me. It seemed like he knew, but he didn't want to say. So we prayed, and that was that. A month later, it was April 20, 2007, Tish did his normal routine of taking the girls to school while I headed off to work. I felt a strong urge to give him a big hug and a kiss, and then said, "See you later." I got to work and spoke to him briefly like always to make sure the girls were okay. He said he was riding his motorcycle to NY, and he would be back later. He called a few hours later to let me know he was on his way back and was with a couple of friends that were riding as well. That was the last time I heard his voice. The next call came from his friend. All I could hear on the phone was "There was a terrible accident, and Tish flew off his bike and broke a railing on the highway." I started to scream at work. I quickly told my manager, had my family pick up the girls, and rushed to the hospital. I got there to see that they were constantly giving him blood transfusions. I talked to his friend that was there and saw what happened. He said that all he knew was that they were all riding together, and then, all of a sudden, he disappeared, and they saw a ball of fire. He said he came back around and saw him. This friend said that he questioned him to see if he understood who and where he was, and he seemed to be coherent at first before going into a coma.

The year started becoming a year of pain instead of joy. I would walk in his room, and his vitals would go up, and as soon as I left the room, they would go down again. It almost felt like he was struggling to stay here for us, but he really wanted to be with the Lord. The doctor came to me after ten hours of working on him, and he said that he broke his rib in half and had many broken bones. I remember him saying that if he made it, he would be a *vegetable*, and would I be okay with taking care of him for the rest of my life. I said, "I made a vow, and until death do us part, I will do it." The whole family was there, and we were all in such disarray not knowing what was going to come. The obvious was in front of us, but no one wanted to accept it. How did someone in a matter of hours be clinging to life, and how can I deal with the inevitable? I went back to the room, and again his vitals went up. So I stayed and talked and held his hand, selfishly wanting him to stay. *Was it God's plan? Did he want to go?* All questions were going through my head. I went into the hallway and talked to my parents. They started praying for me and the kids. The Holy Spirit was so close. He started speaking to me, saying that He was with me. I went in the room, and I knew what I had to do. I held Tish's hand, kissed his head, and said, "It's okay. You can go home to the Lord." No sooner after that, the doctor came out and told us that he had passed. It was April 21, 2007. We were all distraught. I actually looked up to heaven and said, "God, I don't blame you. Now let me grieve." I then just fell to the ground and fainted. I couldn't believe that this was happening. We were just planning for a big wedding in July, and instead we were planning for a funeral. If I had any enemies, I would never wish this on anyone. This was a hard pill to swallow. I pulled up to the funeral home with his parents to pick out a casket, and I just couldn't handle it, so I ran back to the car. The wake was packed, and my mother's pastor eulogized him. He asked me prior if I wanted an altar call. I said, "Absolutely." This was a home-going service.

Do you know that at his funeral, fifty people accepted Christ as their personal Lord and Savior, including his father! What the enemy meant for evil, God turned in around for His good. Out of the ashes, we rise. The beauty of heaven was at his service. The presence of the Lord was overwhelming (Genesis 50:20). In the moment of deep sadness, my heart was also full of joy. It may not make sense, but so many souls were one for Christ, and that was a huge testimony that God is always present.

My good friend Maulaine donated most of the food from her restaurant and served along with my church members. A few days later, one of the elders visited my home and said that there was an overwhelming peace of God there. She said that she was coming there to encourage me, but she was the one encouraged being there. God is so good that He will really give you the peace that will surpass all human understanding if one's mind stays on Him. Philippians 4:7 says, "And the peace of God, which passeth all understanding, shall keep your hearts and minds through Christ Jesus."

Day after day, different family and friends would stop by to encourage me. I kept holding on to the scripture that an elder gave me to meditate on. Isaiah 54:5 said, "For thy maker is thy husband." That short verse helped to get me to that healing place.

Storm Continues

About a few days later, the phone rang and I got a call that one of my young friends lost his battle with leukemia. It was so difficult to yet see another good person close to me go. He was only in his early twenties. It just didn't seem fair or right that he lost a long fight and battle to a horrid disease. After just burying my husband, I found myself yet again at another funeral. Then the Lord started to show me that I had friends that had already been through losing their spouses. One of my friends was there for me, and she lost her husband three years ago. Another one just lost her husband six months prior and showed up to my house with a bouquet of flowers even though she was grieving herself. I was so in awe at how the Lord loved me that He would send people in my inner circle to comfort me as I comfort them back. It is so important to look at your circle and see who can help you as well as who you can help.

The year that I thought would bring so much happiness seemed like nothing but pain and heartache. Then one day I was at church and my pastor's wife came to me and said she really needed to introduce me to somebody. I met a young lady that just lost her husband as well; however, she was in the car with him. He died in the accident, and she was alive. The family blamed her. Here I was, grieving a month later, and this woman's story seemed far more heart-wrenching than mine. I prayed, cried, and encouraged her. We kept in touch for a while, and I advised her to not lose heart. "God will always use your story for His glory, to encourage and uplift someone else, even when you are going through your own storm."

Maulaine and I became even closer friends. She would call me all the time to check up on me, help watch Destiny, and just be a good friend to me. It was the beginning of June 2007 and I asked Maulaine to watch Destiny for me so she agreed to watch her at her newly opened restaurant. I came to pick her up, but Maulaine would offer me food as always, and we would sit and talk. This time one of her good friends were there, and she kept telling him about my story of 9/11 and how my husband just passed. So I started to share with him my story. Then Maulaine said to me, "What do you think happens when a person dies?"

I replied, "I believe that when a person dies, if they are in Christ, one door closes and the other opens to eternity. However, if you are not in Christ, well…not so nice."

I then went on to say that "I really didn't think the person that was passing felt the pain like we did."

The conversation was a little strange, but there was a peaceful presence of the Holy Spirit around us.

My company at that time would always have free lunch catered every Wednesday, and I asked them to try Maulaine's new restaurant to help her obtain business, and they agreed. She was so excited. It was her first big catering event with a corporate company.

The morning of June 21, 2007, I got a call from Maulaine, and she was saying that she was going to be there early. Unfortunately, I had a field trip that day with my daughter to a farm so I was going to miss it, but I asked one of my coworkers to save me a plate for the next day. Lunch time passed and I got calls from my coworkers of how professional she was as well as how good the food tasted. I called Maulaine and shared the good news; she was so happy that everything went well.

The Dark Road

It was a long day at the farm with a bus full of kids. My phone rang, and it was my sister Amayae.

She replied, "Where are you?"

"On a field trip with Destiny. Why?" I responded.

"Well, I will just wait until you get home," she said.

"What happened," I asked.

I was already a little anxious because it was the second month anniversary of my husband's passing. She replied, "Now is not a good time."

I said, "Amayae, please tell me what is going on." The suspense was killing me.

She said, "Tamyka, I am sorry to say, but Maulaine was just murdered in her restaurant."

I yelled out a loud scream; I thought I startled everyone.

I was like "How, why? I just spoke to her. That can't be true. She just delivered food to my workplace."

She said, "It is all over the news. Someone came into her restaurant and shot her up."

I said, "I don't believe you."

I hung up the phone and called her, and it just kept ringing and ringing. Here came this pain again. *Why, God, why?* I asked myself. The one friend that I could connect to was taken away. I was so angry, hurt, disgusted, lonely, and so many other feelings were combined. Maulaine was such a sweet soul. To be honest, to this day, I don't fully know if I ever really came to grips with what happened to her because it just didn't make sense to me. Yet again, there was another funeral in 2007. When I actually counted, there were seven people that were close to me that lost their lives that year. Instead of anticipating the good things for 2007, I couldn't wait for it to be over and done with. The pain was too much to bear, but I still didn't blame God. I just didn't understand why this all was happening. I felt like Job.

> Job's sons and daughters were having a feast in the home of his oldest son, when someone rushed up to Job and said, "While your servants were plowing with your oxen, and your donkeys were nearby eating grass, a gang of Sabeans attacked and stole the oxen and donkeys! Your other servants were killed, and I was the only one who escaped to tell you." That servant was still speaking, when a second one came running up and saying, "God sent down a fire that killed your sheep and your servants. I am the only one who escaped to tell you." Before that servant finished speaking, a third one raced up and said, "Three gangs of Chaldeans attacked and stole your camels! All of your other servants were killed, and I am the only one who escaped to tell you." That servant was still speaking, when a fourth one dashed up and said, "Your children were having a feast and drinking wine at the home of your oldest son, when suddenly a windstorm from the desert blew the house down, crushing all of your children. I am the only one who escaped to tell you." When Job heard this, he tore his clothes and shaved his head because of his great sorrow. He knelt on the ground, then worshiped God and said: "We bring nothing at birth; we take nothing with us at death. The Lord alone gives and takes. Praise the name of the Lord!" (Job 1:13-21)

In spite of everything, Job did not sin or accuse God of doing wrong. I held on to the promises of the Lord and kept believing and worshipping and not giving in to any evil thoughts. I would press even harder to continue in worship. Honestly, it was because I truly felt that Jesus was the only one that could truly heal my broken heart. Psalm 147:3 said, "He heals the brokenhearted and binds up their wounds."

As I started to draw closer to the Lord, it seemed like more things started to happen. What I didn't expect, was fear and doubt creeping in. I had so much anxiety. Death was always on my mind, because I felt that was all I was faced with. No one knew the darkness I was in, because I masked it well with smiling and always there for everyone. I was afraid to do anything, travel, fly, etc. When people I loved would leave my presence or travel, I would fear they wouldn't return. The trauma was too much to bear. I was thinking of everyone else, and not facing my demons to make others happy. However, the one person I forgot was me. I started to eating heavily to mask the hurt and pain that was deep down inside. I became very angry. Not at God, but just not being able to properly process what I was feeling inside. It seemed as if I was a target for pain and misery. I felt as if everyone around me looked as if I was living this terrible life, and I deserved all this heartache. I couldn't breathe. I told myself that I would never want to marry again, because I didn't want to experience that pain. It was an emotional rollercoaster ride. The devil whispered in my ear via a manager at work saying, "I am going to stay away from you, because you are cursed." It really wasn't a nice thing to say to someone that was heavily grieving, and needed comfort. As much I knew the Word, I couldn't believe it was meant for me. I thought that my sins were what caused me to be in the state. There were times I didn't want to go out the house or be around anyone, but Destiny. I didn't know how to show love anymore. The more people would get close to me, I would find a way to push them away, because I was afraid of losing them. When you lose so many people that you love, it takes a toll on you. Processing the pain is not an easy task, and I surely didn't know how to. I wanted to love again, but I just didn't know how to. So instead, I would lash out at people that I loved so that they wouldn't get too close to me. However, I must say that staircase of unbearable heat on September 11th was a great reminder to me of how I would never want to hurt myself or deny God, because I know hell is much hotter. It's nowhere anyone should want to go. I needed help. I cried out to Jesus to heal my heart from all this pain and misery. I remember when one of my friends came to my house after my husband died, and said, "Wow you are fat". Out of everything a person could say, they said that to me. I was so angry, but looked in the mirror and said to myself, "She is right". I knew that I needed help, because food became my addiction. It was starting to show on my body what was going on inside. I had to do something. I started asking the Lord to show me what to do. He started showing me how to change what I was eating. Then the gym became one of my favorite places. My sister and I started taking ballroom dance class lessons. She didn't know at the time, but I started to feel better about myself. I felt that purpose was still there. Despite all this change, I still didn't want to marry again. That was the vow I made to myself.

As different situations start coming up in life, seeing the plane land on the Hudson and a photo op of the president's plane coming toward our building, I was literally done living in New Jersey, and I desired to move back to Florida for a change. It was then the year of 2010, and I started applying for many jobs hoping that I could get that break. I was slowly seeing all my family moving back to Florida and wanting that same opportunity. It was the summertime, and it didn't seem as if it was going to happen for me transitioning. Therefore, I began to look for apartments further in south New Jersey and just accepted the fact that I was not going anywhere. Well, I got a phone call, and I remember her saying that she came across my resumé and thought that I would be a good fit. I did a phone interview with her, and it was the end of July. Then I received a phone call from the hiring manager, and I had a phone interview with three different people. It looked promising. Maybe Florida would really happen again for me because change was what I needed. They called me to fly down to have a personal interview, and of course I accepted. In a matter of a month, I got the job, and God answered my prayers. I was living in Florida. This was a time for fresh start and new beginnings of my life. I was able to share my testimony at my sisters' church, woman conference, other churches, news station, and many more outlets. Many people were and are still blessed by what God had done in my life. I was able to encourage and uplift people while they were hurting. I continued to understand that, instead of asking God why, I asked who needed my story for His glory. I realized that it was all about the kingdom and living an eternal life.

> In fact, everyone who wants to live a godly life in Christ Jesus will be persecuted, while evildoers and impostors will go from bad to worse, deceiving and being deceived. But as for you, continue in what you have learned and have become convinced of, because you know those from whom you learned it, and how from infancy you have known the Holy Scriptures, which are able to make you wise for salvation through faith in Christ Jesus. (2 Timothy 3:12–15)

The change of scenery was what was well needed. I began working at my company, and everything was going great. I was also able to see my family more frequently, which was an added bonus for Destiny and me. Every day, I would go to the gym even more to try to also change my outer appearance since gaining weight from depression. I was on the treadmill, and wow in walked a man with all those muscles. I was like *He look so good, but he didn't even blink an eye at me.* I had on a scarf and unlike many other gym people, I didn't go to the gym to be seen but to achieve a goal. I didn't expect anyone to look at me.

One day, I was in our company's kitchen talking to one of my coworkers and guess who walked by. I couldn't believe it. The same guy from the gym was working at my company. My heart was in my throat. I just looked, but he looked so mean and serious, yet so handsome to me. I felt a brush of the Holy Spirit, and then that was that. I worked in the office, and he worked in our welding area, so I never really saw him often.

The Shift

It was then the spring of 2012, and my company was having our picnic. Of course, Mr. Gorgeous was there, but with his two sons. I came with Destiny and my little dog. The music came on, and I wanted to dance. I remember clearly what was playing, the Wobble Baby. He came over to me, and my heart was racing. He asked me if I wanted him to watch my dog so I could dance. I wanted to say, "Sure, you can watch me dance," but I didn't. So I gave him the leash for my dog and proceeded to dance. I would wobble harder just to get his attention, and he looked back with a nice smile. Finally, he noticed me, but the song was over. I said, "Thank you," and the dream was over.

The next day at work, my coworker came up to me and said that there was a guy that kept asking about me. I said, "Really, who?"

She said, "Henry Silva."

I exclaimed, "I don't know who that is."

Then I asked her to describe him to me. She began to say he was a Spanish with black hair, looked a little Chinese and had a lot of muscles. I couldn't believe it. The same guy that I saw at the gym for two years straight wanted my phone number. I didn't hesitate at all.

"Please give him my number," I said.

He called, and I didn't expect that his accent would be heavy, but I instantly felt a connection with him. We talked and talked. We went dancing on our first date. Then we began to see each other more frequently and went on dates often while keeping it a secret at work, just in case it didn't work out.

We spent holidays together with our kids and family, and it was great. It was in a duration of four years, and Henry and I just built deeper relations with one another. We even went to church together. He loved the Lord more than me, and he told me his story as a divorced single father. I couldn't believe that God placed me with someone that loved Him liked I loved Him.

One December evening, my family was planning a party at my house, and all my family was there as well as all of Henry's friends. My sisters took me for a ride, and then I got a call from Henry asking why I was taking so long to come back. Little did I know that, that night in December 24, 2015, it would change my life forever. I walked to the backyard and there was a trail of rose petals, and all my family was standing, clapping their hands to see a big sign saying, "Will you marry me"? *What, s this real?* I thought. *Could this be true? How could this dream of mine come true? Why is God blessing me like this?* Of course, I said yes as he asked on his knees and all my loved ones were there to witness the scene. I started to think back as a little girl wanting to learn Spanish, and then I practiced my entire life in and out of school before I even knew Henry. I also remembered the Lord telling me that I would one day marry a Spanish man. I didn't realize that when I took the step and chance to move back to Florida, life would set me up for what God had in store for me. The burnt ashes from all my hurt and pain didn't hurt any longer, and I did rise. Isaiah 61:3 said, "To all who mourn in Israel, he will give a crown of beauty for ashes, a joyous blessing instead of mourning, festive praise instead of despair. In their righteousness, they will be like great oaks that the Lord has planted for his own glory."

It took a year of planning, and on December 23, 2016, Henry and I became husband and wife. That day was so beautiful. Well, it started out raining at first, but I didn't fret. I believed that my outdoor wedding would be beautiful. I trusted that God would hold back the rain at the appointed time, and He surely did. Psalm 37:4 said, "Delight yourself in the Lord, and He will give you the desires of your heart."

The enemy tried to rob me by trying to take away my peace and joy by sending all these storms my way. When you say yes to following Jesus, you will face trial and tribulation, but it is so comforting to know that Jesus already overcame them. Was it easy to go through and still go through difficult times? "These things I have spoken to you, that in Me you may have peace. In the world you will have tribulation, but be of good cheer, I have overcome the world" (John 16:33). Absolutely, it was not, but when you know that you have Jesus on your side, the road is more bearable. He is everything that He says He is to you. He was and is still more than a friend to me. I would not have been able to face all of this without Him walking with me. It wasn't my husband that brought me joy, it was the joy of the Lord that did. I became complete in the Lord, and He sent so many blessings after including my daughter, stepsons, and husband. Everyday, Henry is always expressing and reminding me of his love for me. I never in all my years thought that I would experience love like this after so much trauma.

My brother and his wife have three beautiful children. It does not mean we have forgotten Akil, but God has been good to us. Perspective is very important in walking in trials and tribulations. We know that every day isn't going to be easy; however, we can make the decision to overcome our trials and tribulations with the help of the Holy Spirit. So many people had stories of 9/11 and where God was that day. He was right there as He would be today. He turned a situation that could've been worse into a better one by providing calmness during the storm. The most important thing that we can do is focus on the problem solver instead of the problem. Nothing that I went through or go through was easy. I just learned how to shift my perspective and see God in everything. It didn't mean that the situation was horrible or hard to get over, it just meant that I couldn't get through it on my own. God has surrounded me with a great family, church family, and friends, but more importantly, I am taking my ashes and helping others to rise. We also must understand that seeking professional counseling, is wise as well. Often times, people tend to relate that to crazy or negatively. In actuality, it is good to express your thoughts to a trusted professional, even cry. It does not make you weak, but strong. The Lord says, when you are weak, He is strong. II Corinthians 12:10 "Therefore I take pleasure in infirmities, in reproaches, in needs, in persecutions, in distresses, for Christ's sake. For when I am weak, then I am strong." See God doesn't allow things to happen to hurt us, but He allows it for us to see His glory and to help others to get to Him as well. It is better to give help than to receive it. I didn't necessarily like all the pain that I went through, but it had helped so many that I was honored to be used as His vessel of honor. Like Job, he lost so much, but God gave him double for his trouble. I not only got a second chance at marriage, my daughter, gained two sons, more family, and a house as well. God is truly amazing.

As years passed from the awful experiences, I noticed that God was always sending people my way that I would share my story. To my surprise, they went through similar situations, and sometimes worst. However, they lacked in faith in Lord. I realized that we all have unfortunate experiences that we go through. It is always for someone else that needs Him more. I have put aside my feelings, to see the hurt and lost healed. This is the heart of God, I believe, He died for our sins and iniquities.

> After Job had prayed for his friends, the Lord restored his prosperity and doubled his former possessions. All his brothers and sisters and prior acquaintances came and dined with him in his house. They consoled him and comforted him over all the adversity that the Lord had brought upon him. And each one gave him a piece of silver and a gold ring. So the Lord blessed Job's latter days more than his first. He owned 14,000 sheep, 6,000 camels, 1,000 yoke of oxen, and 1,000 female donkeys. And he also had seven sons and three daughters. He named his first daughter Jemimah, his second Keziah, and his third Keren-happuch. No women as beautiful as Job's daughters could be found in all the land, and their father granted them an inheritance among their brothers. After this, Job lived 140 years and saw his children and their children to the fourth generation. And so Job died, old and full of years. (Job 42:10–17)

When people heard of Job, they thought of the bad and the good. He lost many, but he regained double for his trouble. Out of all the ashes that were in my life, God used and was still using my story for His glory so that people would rise. When the Lord commanded us to go out and make disciples out of men, it came with some setbacks and disappointments, but I was reminded that we would win in the end. I have learned over my own personal trials and tribulations is to ask God who instead of why so that I could be used as His vessel to help advance the kingdom of heaven. The pain will always exist, but I live on purpose now for the cause of Jesus Christ.

We should all take inventory of our lives. I challenge you to make two columns. In one side write down everything that is going good in your life. Next, write down everything that is going wrong. I guarantee there is more good than bad. God never told us when we say Yes to Him, that we wouldn't face trials and tribulations. However, we can take all the ashes out, and Rise. Pray that God will direct you to the person that share similar story, and needs Him more than you, so that you can be a living witness of His love towards mankind. It is time for us to come out of the ashes, and RISE.

What Next

So what is next? How can you rise in your ashes?

1. Pray and pray some more, even if all you can say is thank you Jesus. I guarantee He will be there.

2. It is normal to grieve, don't let anyone have you believing you need to be strong. The bible clearly tells us, when we are weak, he is strong. The Lord take pleasure in comforting our hearts at all times.

3. Find a trusted person that you can share with, that will not only cry with you, but encourage you so you don't stay in a depressed state.

4. Ask the Lord to show you a person or people that are going through the same things as you, and look to lean on and help one another to Rise.

5. Forgive, forgive, and forgive. Don't blame yourself or others, but learn to forgive and let God heal your heart.

6. Stay away from negativity.

7. Read all of God's promises in his word for your life. There are many people in the bible that are relatable.

8. Don't feel guilty about moving on and living. It doesn't mean that you forget about your past; however, you can use your story to spread God's glory.

9. Don't give up. Keep pressing forward, knowing that God is good, and he is always there even in our darkest moments.

10. Pray, live, love, and laugh. Don't be afraid to pray, live, love or laugh. It is healing to the mind, body, and soul.

There is not one person that can say that they haven't experienced any ashes in their life. The definition for ashes is the remains after burning. We remain after going through different things. Take those difficult circumstances and situations, and rise up out of those ashes. It is time for you to rise and shine with His light.

About the Author

My wife, Tamyka Silva was born in New Jersey and raised in South Florida where we currently live with our kids. Her parents are from Jamaica and currently reside in the United States. She has a tight bond with all of her siblings. Over the past 20 years, she has worked in the Information Technology field. She holds four degrees, Associates in Applied Science in Telecommunications Management, BA in Education, and dual Masters in Information Systems and Project Management.

She enjoys dancing, the great outdoors, and fitness. She finds comfort in spending time with her family at home, vacation, as well as going to the beach. Tamyka is Zumba certified, and loves to assist people in attaining their fitness goals. She is a proud member of Delta Sigma Theta Sorority Inc.

Tamyka has a passion for Christ and spreading the good news of His love towards people. She is always finding ways to encourage and uplift people to be a better version of themselves. Her humble and sociable character captivates people in wanting to be around her. Tamyka sees everyone equally no matter their background, status, or economic situation/surplus. She is always trying to give back to the community, and letting the light within her shine.

CPSIA information can be obtained
at www.ICGtesting.com
Printed in the USA
BVHW052249300919
559810BV00023BA/1887/P